The Bedsitting Room

The contents of this book defies description, so don't expect me to tell you what it's about. It's that tremendously successful play which was first staged at the Mermaid Theatre in 1963, moved on to the Duke of York's and the Comedy, and then took off round the country. If you never saw the play, now's your chance to find out what happened after Lord Fortnum changed into a Bedsitting Room as the result of a nuclear holocaust. And if you did see the play—well, you still want to find out.

I think you'd better buy a copy and read it, or ask at your library, or borrow it, but best of all, buy it because if you borrow it you won't give it back, and you'll feel guilty and you'll lose a friend or get fined so **buy it and read it.**

By Spike Milligan

THE LITTLE POT-BOILER

A BOOK OF BITS OR A BIT OF A BOOK

A DUSTBIN OF MILLIGAN

THE BEDSIDE MILLIGAN

Tandem editions 25p

The Bedsitting Room

Spike Milligan and John Antrobus

Introduced by
Bernard Miles

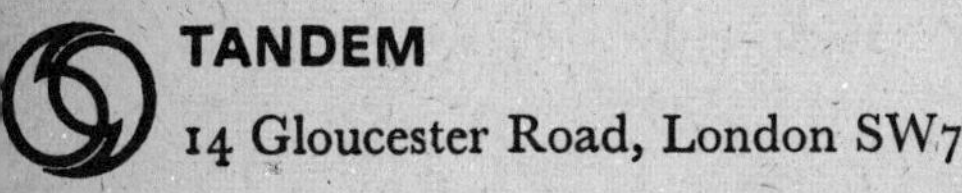

TANDEM
14 Gloucester Road, London SW7

First published in Great Britain by Margaret and Jack Hobbs, 1970
Published by Universal-Tandem Publishing Co. Ltd, 1972

Original Cast List

Captain Pontius Kak	Graham Stark
Lord Fortnum of Alamein	Valentine Dyall
Mate/Arthur Scroake	Spike Milligan
Shelter Man	John Bluthal
Plastic Mac Man	John Bluthal
Underwater Vicar	John Bluthal
Brigadier/Sergeant	John Bluthal
Chest of Drawers/Gladys Scroake	Marjie Lawrence
Penelope	Marjie Lawrence
Diplomat	Bob Todd
First Announcer	Bob Todd
Sea Captain	Bob Todd
Second Announcer	Johnny Vyvyan
Delivery Man/Chauffeur	Johnny Vyvyan
Seaman	Johnny Vyvyan
Coffin Man	Clive Elliott
Pianist	Alan Chase
Third Announcer	Bill Kerr
EXTRAS	
Phantom	
Old Soldier	
Orderly	

Music played by the Temperance Seven

Act 1 Captain Pontius Kak's surgery and Government surplus store

Act 2 Scene 1 Lord Fortnum, the room
Scene 2 Lord Fortnum, the well known room

There should be one interval of 15 minutes

Original production directed and designed by Spike Milligan and John Antrobus

Music arranged by Cliff Bevan

Intraducshun

So I rang Spike an sed wat about a staj play for us sum-time. An he sed wot with orl these fred scripts on my plate, sum opes. But he sed there iz wun of our lads as a gud ideer for a staj play an e mite rite you wun, iz name is John Antrobus, and i wil sen him roun ter see you, so i sed rite.

An I sed i eer you av got an ideer for a staj play, an he sed that iz rite. An he sed it is about a man oo gets changed into er bedsitin room. And I sed that souns vry promisin an i would like yeu to get rite doun an rite it for us. And i pade him wot is corld an advarnse, which iz sumthin ter be going on with, an orf he went and I never seed the culer of im agen fer 9 munths.

An then he cum roun an sed he woz getin on with it, an I sed abowt time to! An orf he went agen, an it woz anuthr 7 munths bifor I seed im a gen. An then he sed it woz cumin on an I sed wood you lik a bit mor ter be getin on with an he sed no i am orlrite.

An then cum Treshur Iland time, larst crismus but wun, an Spike woz Bengun the best that ever woz or wilbee, tho i sey it muself who am a carikteracter, an a vry jelus wun an envyus too! God fergive me! An sudnly ther wos John and Spike in Spikz dresin rume with the dor lokd an a tipriter goin like mad. Thowz of yeu oo no Treshur Iland will reeliz the part of Bengun iz a short wun, rite in the midl of the play, mor lik a lekcher. An there is plenti of time orl roun it for the acter to do somthin els besids. So there woz John an Spike typriterin awa lik mad in Spikz dresin rume, an showtin at eechuther, an Spike woz bangin the tabel. An wen I tuk them in ther foud, an sum paper, an sum noo tipriterin ribins, ther wox Spike on th flawr compozin, an John woz compozin bak at im an typriterin it doun. And it got to such a pich I had ter go owt of th roum becos they wood not be gainsed. An I arskd if thay wood lik sum mor muni to be goin on with, but John sed no pis orf! So orf I pist! I am sorry to be rood but thats how it woz an I no yeu wil want the trooth, wich iz sed to be more preshus than roobiz.

An thats how th bedsitin room got dun. An it woz tride owt at Kantrbry at a theatr cald the Marlow an Mister Tynan oo rites the peesix in the 'Observar' went doun an give it iz akerlade, wich is considered enuf fer any play in all conshuns. An now it is here, but not the same, becoz it is biger an they have put in a lot mor stuff to mak it betr, an we hope it wil now be orlrite.

Plees do not think John an Spike ar wikid men oo rite such stuf. An plees do not think we are wikid pepel for putin it on. Reely they luv england, an th pools, an th old aj penshuners, an parliment, an Misis Topham, an the TUC, ancetra, ancetra. An John woz at Sandherst, an that iz wear he lernt a lot of the stuf that iz in thiz play, but no wun nos wear Spike lernt wot he lernt cos he iz vry uneddikated man with a big sole . . . a bit to big if yu arsk me! An sumtimes you feel lik kickin im up the arse, but yoo wil be glad to heer he still has as much hope as will cuver a sixpence. So God bless yoo orl an joly gud luk.

p.s. So you see it woz reely comishund, an rote, an racked owt heer, an partley brawt to bein, an we ar prowd to be wun of its consideribel midwyvs.

p.p.s. An I shud tell yeu it neerly ment a sizarian!

Bernerd Miles

Prop List

Portable parking meter, top practical with click effect.
Giant DAZ packets slung on gas mask belt.
Tin mug.
Roll of lavatory paper, ordinary.
Comb.
Giant Lux packet on gas mask belt.
Milk bottle, full, with gold top.
ARP helmet.
Gas mask, canister type.
Rifle.
Insect spray gun, with coloured mist.
8 ft 9 in high constructed pile of boots, then pile of boots on top to give added height, these boots will be removed before striking Union Jack on top.
Step ladder to get to top of pile of boots.
Brochure or pamphlet.
Jayne Mansfield.
Blankets.
Victorian hat-stand.
Telephone set, no wires, just receiver. Green and modern.
Birth certificate strapped to wrist
Punishment caps, design from D. Jones. Each with flashing light on top, green, fellow and red. Batteried and switched.
Union Jack handkerchief.
Defeat of England Medal, ordinary medal.
Chalk.
Statue of Queen Victoria to go in niche at side of stage.
Flip top Bible, made like cigarette pack.
Starting pistol.
Victorian brass bed, no rail at foot end.
Patchwork quilt.
White sheets.
Telescopes. (One for Vicar, long, and one inside coffin.)
Diplomatic bag with document, yellow and black seal on, chained to wrist.
Bath chair with handle running out of back

centrally, on handle a steering wheel.
Iron mangle with handle and practical.
Never-ending sock to go through mangle.
Yacht to appear out of coffin through hole, on stick and with yellow flag.
Hot-water bottle, red rubber.
Portable door, with blackboard panel for writing on. Design with D. Jones.
Suitcases and brown-paper bags.
Large pair black scissors.
Baby's rattle. Blue.
Ship's telegraph and with sound.
Moses basket.
Magnifying glass, 4 in across.
Chicken. Real
Carving set.
Lantern, council type with red for danger. Batteried on switch.
Noses false with moustaches.
Head mask to give the impression another person is on the TV screen.

10
Heavy knife.
Washing blanket.
Prow of ship to be fitted round S. Milligan's waist.
Eye patch.
Coffin with hinge lid, deep. Holes in lid for yacht already mentioned, hole in side for balloons, space for bailer and container of water. To hold a TV aerial and whole thing painted black.
Fob watch on 6 pt of chain.
Fly swatter, plactic and red and yellow.
Cigar box, with plastic coloured clothes pegs.
Ring setting for 'bread stone'.
Notebook and pencil.
Visiting cards.
Sign, reading 'Refined room to let', to fit portable window pane.
Chocolate gold-wrapped pennies.
Doctor's reflex hammer.
Brick for Fortnum, to be inside coat in pocket and easy to drop out.

Glove on never-ending sleeve for Fortnum, grey, to run into pocket inside coat having travelled through armhole.

Exigencies of space preclude listing all the props.

THE BEDSITTING ROOM

ACT ONE

Back projection of moving (but silent) film of explosion of H-bomb at an atoll. Taken from the sea level, then from the air. Sound with the above : A baby cooing in its pram. Black out.

Spotlight on piano. Enter PIANIST on rostrum wearing evening dress. PIANIST talks gibberish as though announcing what he will play. He then sings 'When the Lights go on again all over the World' (at the same time accompanying himself on piano). During songs, large placard is lowered from above with the words : BUDDHISTS USE ESSO! (Try to use the same typography as the Esso signs use.) This placard obscures the PIANIST. There enters a man in black cloak, black hat, with a long pole on the end of which is affixed a white-gloved pointing finger, the index finger being larger than necessary and slightly bulbous at the tip. He also sings in harmony with the PIANIST. A second placard is lowered advertising . . .

Before each placard is lowered the PHANTOM shouts

PHANTOM : Lower Awayyyyyyyyyyyy ! ! !

and points to the placards.

He then walks to a charred black tree, the branches of which appear to have grown barbed wire; in its branches is a black-headed vulture. The PHANTOM opens a small door in tree, inserts a key, winds up (sound of winding), then prods the vulture.

PHANTOM : Come on little birdie.

Sound : A sweet twittering noise is heard.
Voice over loudspeaker interrupts all the proceedings.

VOICE : Ladies and gentlemen, the curtain will be rising in one minute. Will you kindly take your seats.

The effect of this announcement on the man in black coat is to make him break down in dismay and exits crying.
The placards are flown.
Black out.

Sound over P.A. : 'Housewives' Choice Music'.
From inside the pyramid of boots, the light is faded up, showing translucent red. Stage lights come up. Enter stage right CAPTAIN PONTIUS KAK. He wears a brown overall and a 'Macmillan Moscow hat' (under his overall he wears officer K.D. hot climate uniform, long trousers), has a small portable transistor radio slung over his shoulder. Carries a small, rigid, hand-held Union Jack. He climbs up the ladder against the side of the boots. Plants the Union Jack.

KAK : (*to audience*) Why? Because it was *there* !

Sound over P.A. : 'Housewives' Music' stops. Three pips. Pause. PONTIUS KAK hits the radio. It emits another pip.

GIRL UNDERSTUDY : (*microphone side stage over the P.A.*) This is the Radio Caroline Service of the BBC. The time is ten-thirty and here is the news read by Mrs Wedgwood Benn. Parliament resumes its debate on debates about questions and quosthions were asked. Mr Fnockington Crapologies asked the Defence Secretary : 'Who was that lady I saw you with last night?' The Minister declined to answer and said: 'The matter is being looked into.' Mr Wilson, Prime Minister of no fixed politics, then made the following statement.

SPIKE: On this the first anniversary of the Nuclear Misunderstanding which led to World War Three, I'd like to point out that under a Labour Administration, this was the shortest World War on record, two minutes twenty-eight seconds precisely, including the signing of the Peace Treaty, which is now on sale at Her Majesty's Stationery Office. The—er—the—er—Great Task of burying our forty-eight million dead was carried out with cheerfulness and good-will, so characteristic of the Labour Party. When this terrible incident occurred, I was at the UNO Disarmament Conference with President Johnson. I flew home immediately and was greeted on the steps of No 10 by a Mr Breznief . . . who invited me in. There followed some pretty hard bargaining and he finally agreed to fix the rent of No 10 at an undisclosed figure of Bloody Incomes Policy I . . . I want my tea . . .

Sound off of obvious coconut shells: impressions of horse approaching.

MATE: Whoa back, whoa . . .

Enter LORD FORTNUM. He is dressed in a silk black top hat, with a Revolving Radar Scanner *protruding from the top. Long, tatty, velvet-collared black overcoat, wearing a Harrow tie, white shirt, striped City trousers; from the knees down his legs are covered with newspapers held in place by string. Slung over his shoulder is a large packet of Lux. He pulls a portable (on wheels) shop window, mid stage in front of the pile of boots. FORTNUM peers through the shop window, he takes a fish from under his arm, holds it up and says (in the grand manner)*

FORTNUM: Ah! *This* must be the Plaice! (*Aside*) Not my favourite opening line actually. *My* favourite is 'Lady Teasdale by all that's damnable!' Yes, I'll try that.

Holds up fish.

FORTNUM: (*aside*) I prompt!

BOB TODD: (*off*) Lady Teasdale by all that's damnable!

FORTNUM: What? That's my line!

Note: The fish is the length of an umbrella, and has an umbrella handle protruding from out of its mouth. FORTNUM taps on shop window to attract KAK's attention.

FORTNUM: I say you — you up here . . .

KAK looks down at FORTNUM: from here on, whoever is BEHIND *the shop front window (that is, up stage) always mimes the words of his dialogue.*

KAK: (*mime*) Did you call me?

FORTNUM: Can you come here . . .

KAK: (*descends ladder*) I can't hear what you're saying . . .

FORTNUM: Are you Captain Pontius Kak?

KAK is now right behind the window and is miming that he cannot hear.

FORTNUM : (*shouting*) Are you . . . Oh, it's no good, I can't hear a . . .

He walks behind the window. At the same time KAK comes to the front of the window.

KAK : . . . Oldest consenting male adult?

FORTNUM : (*shouting in mime*) For God's sake. I'm trying to find out who you are.

KAK : I wonder if he's saying happiness is egg shaped?

KAK opens the door in between the shop windows : immediately we hear FORTNUM in mid-sentence.

FORTNUM : . . . is egg shaped!

KAK : Please don't stand out there shouting — people will talk.

FORTNUM is entering.

FORTNUM : Sorry. Are you—er—Captain Pontius Kak?

KAK : Yes. Pronounced *Kak* as in 'You dirty swine'.

FORTNUM : Good. I've been advised to come and see you.

KAK : Certainly — which part would you like to see first?

FORTNUM : Preferably me.

KAK: Good, now do you want Psychiatry or Army Surplus?

FORTNUM: Both, I want Surplus Army Psychiatry.

KAK: Go Oooooooo

FORTNUM: OOOOOOOOO

KAK puts his own finger in FORTNUM'S mouth and wobbles it.

KAK: Anything else?

FORTNUM: Yes, a small brown loaf.

KAK: Don't say Brown, say (Prices and Incomes) Queer.

FORTNUM: (*furtive*) All right, a small Queer Loaf (or Prices and Incomes Loaf).

KAK: You got here just in time.

FORTNUM: Why?

KAK: We haven't got any. Is that your Horse-Drawn Rolls outside?

FORTNUM: I suppose it's all right to say yes?

KAK: Yes.

FORTNUM: Yes, I acquired it from Lord Montague; he just bought a horse-drawn Mercedes from Lord Snowden.

KAK: Not *the* Lord Snowden?

FORTNUM: No, *a* Lord Snowden.

KAK : Ah ! The woods are full of them. Now—er—I didn't quite catch your name.

FORTNUM : My card (*Pronounces 'M'Card'. Hands card across*)

KAK : MacCard? Scotsman, eh? Wait, this card's blank.

FORTNUM : Yes, I suffer from loss of memory. Actually my name's on the back.

KAK : Damn silly place to have it printed.

FORTNUM : I let one side for advertising.

KAK : (*turns card*) Ahh. Lord Fortnum of Alamein?

FORTNUM : Yes, I bought the title off an old soldier who found himself on hard times.

KAK : (*looks at FORTNUM's radar topper*) Did the hat go with it?

FORTNUM : No no, this is the new four-minute early-warning hat. It—er—it (*gleefully*) gives you that extra minute in bed.

KAK : (*pause. Looks*) Yes. Step into the Surgery, will you?

FORTNUM steps into a white chipped enamel wash basin which is centre stage next to couch. KAK walks around FORTNUM.

KAK : Now answer these questions. Do you think sleeping alone is contagious?

FORTNUM : I don't know. I've never had it.

KAK : Right, now let's have you up on the couch.

FORTNUM lies on a couch; a feather is suspended over his midriff from a coiled wire attached to side of couch. KAK agitates the feather.

KAK : This self-same couch was invented by one of the Earls of Warwick, for some strange . . . *foul and perverted reason* ! ! ! ! !

As he says the last sentence he becomes obsessed and trembles. FORTNUM leaps from the couch holding his trousers.

FORTNUM : Now see here ! There's a limit to what I'll do.

KAK : Well, we'll go as far as that then, shall we? ? ? ?

FORTNUM grudgingly lies down again. KAK re-agitates the feather.

FORTNUM : . . . I say, it's not unpleasant.

KAK : No, it's only when the convulsions start that—

Here FORTNUM goes to get up.

KAK : There, there. (*Holds him down*) Now . . .

KAK walks to head of the couch, goes to sit on an empty space. At the last moment a DICKENSIAN CLERK holding a chair under himself slides underneath KAK, so that KAK is seated in his lap. This is all done in one smooth movement.

KAK : Now then, start at the beginning, tell me all.

FORTNUM : My paternal ancestor Lord Crapologies Fel de Minge.

KAK : (*quietly without stopping FORTNUM speaking*) Did he?

FORTNUM : What? Came over with the William The Conqueror, first class of course . . . it was Hastings Ten Sixty-six . . .

KAK : (*writes down on pad*) Hastings Ten Sixty Six. Right, I'll phone him later.

FORTNUM : Yes, he'll bear me out. . . . Well, he was a tall man with garnished ginger knees and several ways about him. On Sundays they say he took a spotted woman to church. . . . Now in the late autumn of 1066, during an attack of Coptic Gadfly on the Knack-eeeeee.

KAK : Yes yes, needn't go back *that* far. How do you spell Knack-ee?

FORTNUM : I don't. Could you—er—

KAK : Oh, I'm sorry. (*He re-agitates the feather*) Now tell me something more recent.

FORTNUM : Well if you *must* know, everything was going swimmingly until they dropped this terrible . . .

Sound of mule raspberries. Groans.
Everybody on stage leaps up and starts swiping at invisible

flying things. The PIANIST, who up to now has been reading a paper behind drawn curtains, pulls back the curtains and launches into a furious version of 'When the Lights go on again'. At the same time a SMALL MAN in a leopard skin, Army boots, great ginger wig (and it must be ENORMOUS*) and great red beard, enters with a great club with which he batters the stage in a frenzy. The noise stops, the LITTLE MAN exits in tears. PIANIST pulls the curtains on his platform. All reverts to normal.*

KAK : The H-bomb?

FORTNUM : Yes, that's the one. Ever since then, I've been strangely troubled.

KAK : Did the noise keep you awake?

FORTNUM : No, I slept like a log, I do tree impressions as well. When I came to I discovered a marked change. As was my wont I toddled along for lunch at the Constitutional Club, and it had gone — rubble, nothing but rubble, and such small portions. I saw Lord Hailsham standing outside stark naked waving a Union Jack and shouting 'Vive le Sport'. I could see his membership had lapsed, so I ignored him. I wrote a stiff letter to *The Times,* then, *they* broke the news to me. While I'd been asleep, they'd had World War III. (*Walks forward, looks up*) I didn't get a chance to join the regiment.

KAK : There, there — that part of it came as quite a shock to me too; fortunately I managed to get there in time for a disability pension.

FORTNUM : Well, since the bomb I haven't eaten a thing.

KAK : Why not?

FORTNUM : (*annoyed*) Can't afford it! Bread at sixty-four gns per fine ounce. See this? (*Shows signet ring*) I had this bit of bread mounted this morning.

KAK : Gad, beautifully cut.

FORTNUM removes ring and holds it out to KAK.

FORTNUM : Look, Doctor, all this, if you'll give me a prescription to alleviate malnutrition.

KAK : Right! (*Writes on pad*) T grams Brown Windsor Soup. Eggs and Chips. Jam and Custard. There, I want you to take this three times a day before meals, any good restaurant will make it up.

FORTNUM : I'll try Boots Café . . .

KAK : Good, anything else?

FORTNUM : Yes, ever since they dropped this bomb, I've had the morbid fear I might turn into a Bedsitting Room.

Here the actors must introduce great tension.

KAK : A Bedsitting Room?

FORTNUM : Yes!

KAK : Will you be empty? I—er—I mean—how would you visualise yourself as this Bedsitting Room?

FORTNUM : A brick wall with brick wallpaper over it. A plastic draining board, fluorescent lighting, red bakelite door knobs and an outside wooden karzi. Oh dear, what should I do?

KAK : Well, I think you ought to stick out for thirty shillings a week — at a push you might get two quid.

FORTNUM : Two quids??? Look, you're not getting the point, I don't want to be *a* Bed *Sitting Room.* You can't have a Lord turning into that sort of thing. Woburn Abbey, Blenheim Palace, where the takings are reasonable, but a bed sit at two quids?

KAK : You sound quite *Ad*-Amant about that.

FORTNUM : I am *Ad*-Amant. I am.

KAK : You sound quite Adamant about that *Ad*-Amant.

FORTNUM : *I* am. *I* am. (*Stresses*)

KAK : Look, let's be practical — have you seen a good estate agent?

FORTNUM : Yes. (*Full of meaning*) He was quite quite beautiful.

KAK: (*worried*) What?

FORTNUM: But he refused to handle me until I'd become this blasted Bed Sit. Two quid. The fool didn't realise, I'll do *anything* to stave off the prospect of becoming a Bed Sit. I'll pay anything . . . even . . . (*He produces a gold coin*) . . . even *Money*!

KAK: (*falls on his knees*) Money!

Black out, divine spotlight from directly overhead on KAK. Sound of Hallelujah Chorus by Handel (vocal chorus). FORTNUM gives him the coin, KAK bends his head in relief. Lights up. Music stops. KAK to his feet.

KAK: Well, well, Lord Fortnum, I think we can do business. Roll up your sleeve.

FORTNUM rolls up sleeve.

FORTNUM: Gad! An arm.

KAK: Say Ah.

FORTNUM: Ahhhh.

KAK: Good, you can get dressed again.

FORTNUM turns modestly away to pull down sleeve.

KAK: Now, I want you to start taking these Anti Bed Sit Pills; take six a day, one every half mile.

FORTNUM: But I only live a mile away.

KAK: You'll have to move further out, then.

FORTNUM: But I . . .

Heavy hammering on side door of theatre. In event of there being no side door near stage, a hand protrudes from the wings and beckons KAK. KAK opens the door or reaches the beckoning hand. Immediately a parking meter is thrust in front of him and 'MATE', the parking meter attendant, enters. Old cloth cap, ragged overcoat, zip-up boot slippers, large iron-frame spectacles, old, about fifty-five, unshaven, long hair. He has a packet of Daz slung around his shoulders.

MATE: You can't park here, sir.

He writes a parking ticket, puts it in coffin.

MATE: This should cost him a fortune. I—

He suddenly is taken by the large packet of Lux which LORD FORTNUM has slung around his shoulder. FORTNUM tries to slide the packet out of sight.

MATE: Hold it, hold, hold, what's this then. Ohhhhhh. Wearing Lux in a Daz area. Eh oh ho ho ho ho.

Writes a ticket.

MATE: I shall have to report you to the Daz Committee, sir. Not to mention Bazonka.

FORTNUM: Bazonka?

MATE : I told you not to mention that, sir. I shall have to charge you and give you the following warning. (*Suddenly sings long-drawn-out notes. Sings*)

We're doing the Daz
We're doing the Daz
You get all the dirt off the front of yer shirt with Daz Daz Daz
Whenever you 'as
A packet of Daz
You watch every stain
Go right down the drain
With Daz Daz Daz.
Put it in the Corfee
Put it in the Tea
Rub on your belly and shout

PIANIST : (*from rostrum*) 'Hi diddle dee.'

MATE :

A Razz a Matz
We're doing the Daz.
Keep Paddington White
On a Saturday Night with
Daz Daz Daz.

Black out. Spot on stage. Hanging from the flies is a blond wig. Enter BOB TODD in ankle-length string vest, packet of Daz slung over shoulder. He places a ladder under the wig, ascends ladder and brings his head right into the wig to fit perfectly.

MATE : It's Treade Dick. England's oldest consenting male adult for Smethwick.

SHELTER MAN : Dat's smart, dat's smart. Look what happened to me and my partner. While I was at home, sleeping with his wife, he was in der office robbing the safe. How can you do business wid people like that, eh?

KAK : You a family man?

BOB TODD : (*sings*)
When I was a young man
My vests were always dirty
They remained in that condition
For many many years until I was approximately in the region of shall we say thirty.

He produces a tambourine, rattles it violently without any meaning.

Then one day,
A handsome cross-eyed stranger came my way
He poured white powder on my head
An this is what he saidddddddd.

Lights up.

MATE : (*reprised*)
I baptise thee Daz
A razz a ma tazz
Keep Paddington white
On a Saturday night with

OMNES :
DAZZ! DAZZZ! DAZZZZZ!

MATE : Is that your horse-drawn Rolls parked out there?

FORTNUM : Who wants to know?

MATE : Me. Me.

FORTNUM : Well, listen, Mimi. That horse is a horse of a different colour. And why are you wearing that absurd Russian Soviet hat?

MATE : 'Aven't you 'eard? There's a rumour that the Ruskies are taking over.

Both KAK and FORTNUM produce from their pockets two identical Russian hats.

FORTNUM : Well, let the swines come, we're ready for them, eh? Eh? (*To KAK*) Tovarisch.

MATE : That disguise don't fool me. Why is your Rolls being pulled by a working-class Daz horse?

FORTNUM : Look, that horse is Prince Philip's third cousin.

MATE : I don't care — it's parked on a parking meter.

FORTNUM : Yes, but I put money in it.

MATE : *Money!* . . . (*He falls to his knees and looks up*) 'Ere, they didn't play it that time. Must be for C of E's only. Well, I'm off, must be the hot weather.

Here MATE blows a police whistle that is slung round his neck on string.

MATE: Ah, there's the lunch whistle! I think I'll go and have it in the Daz Peopledrome and watch the traditional mixing of D X 7, the new wonder political whitener — it forces Brown in and Wilson out. Yes, remember, folks.

Reprise of the Daz. Exits.

FORTNUM: Well, there he goes, living proof that there he goes. I must be going.

KAK: Yes, don't worry too much about this Bed Sitting Room —

A red house brick drops from FORTNUM's coat.

FORTNUM: Doctor, I've dropped a brick.

KAK: Then *it's started* . . . you must hurry with those tablets.

FORTNUM: Yes, yes, thank you. What can I say?

KAK: Say, 'How much will that be?'

FORTNUM: (*reeling*) I don't feel well enough to say that, Doctor. (*Romantically*) And Doctor?

KAK: Yes?

Piano arpeggio.

FORTNUM : (*sings*) I'll bring along a smile and a song for everrrr.

KAK and FORTNUM : (*sings*) Only a Rose, IIIII Goveeeeeeeeeeee.

FORTNUM pulls off shop front as they sing. Exits.

KAK : Always a safe exit. Now then . . . see . . . (*Picks up milk bottle. Taps it*) Ah, radiation's falling, should be nice day tomorrow.

Sudden sound of numerous bolts being withdrawn, chains being pulled through iron rings, keys in locks. As the noise continues, KAK starts to search the floor for the point of origin. He feels for a walking-stick. Suddenly a trap door in the floor opens slightly, gradually a MAN emerges dressed in black fedora hat, black jacket, middle-calf-length kilt, with wash brush as a sporran. Hot-water bottle hangs at the back, with a pair of yellow rubber ankle high boots. He carries a bell-mouthed blunderbuss. He doesn't see KAK. He searches the stage. KAK coughs to draw attention. SHELTER MAN revolves, does a little dance and then challenges KAK.

KAK : Good God, a Zen Buddhist.

SHELTER MAN : (*German-Jewish accent*) It is over, then—

KAK : What?

SHELTER MAN : World War Three.

KAK : Oh yes, it was in all the papers.

SHELTER MAN : I get all the papers.

KAK : It was in the Stop Press.

SHELTER MAN : Oh, the one paper I didn't get.

KAK : What's down there, then?

SHELTER MAN : (*indignant*) What's down there? Hyman Schlapper and Sons, Underground Furriers, Model Gowns, Felt Hat Cutters. . . . (*Confidentially*) Tell me how many got killed in the war?

KAK : Forty-nine million.

SHELTER MAN : Oh, are we going to have trouble getting staff. . . . Now den . . . (*Produces his order book*) How many gross of—er—der Gold Lame Cocktail Gowns . . . two, three gross?

KAK : Look, I find this distasteful if you must know, since they dropped the bomb I've stopped wearing them.

SHELTER MAN : Oh, what a pity. Still, be prepared, dat's what I always say, what do you say?

KAK : It's a long road that has no turning.

SHELTER MAN : He who laffs last laffs last.

KAK : Rolling stones gather no moss empires.

MATE : (*leaps in*) I didn't write this bit.

SHELTER MAN : Soo, is this your business den?

KAK : Yes.

SHELTER MAN : Want a partner?

KAK : I am the partner.

SHELTER MAN : Whose partner?

KAK : Mine. I'm Partner and Company.

SHELTER MAN : Yes, dat was der trouble. My wife, all she would do was Buy Buy.

KAK : Buy what?

SHELTER MAN : Black birds. Buy Buy Black Birds.

MATE : (*leaps in*) I didn't write that either.

SHELTER MAN : Mind you, she stopped it when I shot her dead.

KAK : Dead? Sorry to hear that.

SHELTER MAN : My wife died, you know.

KAK : I'm sorry to hear that again.

SHELTER MAN : I'm sorry to say it again . . . never did get a laugh. . . .

KAK : Not the way you say it. . . .

SHELTER MAN : What did you do before they dropped the bomb, then?

KAK : Nothing. I was in the Army.

SHELTER MAN : Oh? What regiment?

KAK : They wouldn't tell, Official Secrets you know. From what I could make of the cap badge, it was the Royal Household Cavalry.

SHELTER MAN : You have to be a householder to get in.

KAK : No. This refers to Buckingham Palace, which alas was totally destroyed by the bomb.

SHELTER MAN : Tsu tsu. (*Takes off his hat. Sings*) God Save Our Gracious King.

KAK : No, no, we don't sing that any more, we now sing God Save Mrs Gladys Scroake. She is the nearest in line to the Throne.

SHELTER MAN : (*sings*) God Save Mrs Gladys Scroake.

KAK joins in and sings.

BOTH : God Save Mrs Gladys Scroake, God Save Gladys Scroake.

SHELTER MAN : So the Royal Family were killed, then.

KAK : (*smiles patriotically*) No, they, a brace of pheasants and Helicopter Jim are safe in Barclays Bank, Australia.

SHELTER MAN : Schalom, oh 'ere. Who—er—who won this war then?

As the SHELTER MAN talks, KAK walks up stage, followed by the SHELTER MAN.

KAK : We don't really know. According to the TAM rating, the Russians have.

SHELTER MAN : (*frightened*) Russians?

He grabs KAK's Russian hat and dons it.

KAK : But then, according to the Daz Warden (*At this point KAK should be standing over the trap door. A pole with a white cowboy Stetson is quickly pushed up to KAK, who takes it, dons it*) the Americans are taking over.

SHELTER MAN pushes up peak of Russian hat and puts a cigar in mouth. Assumes a gum-chewing American attitude.

SHELTER MAN : Americans? OK OK OK. Then if you don't know who won, who lost?

KAK : Oh, England lost. It was our turn, you know.

Suddenly KAK starts to walk briskly around the stage. He walks off prompt side followed by SHELTER MAN, reappears followed by STRING VEST MAN, they walk behind pile of boots, reappear followed by MAN in red beard and leopard skin, disappear other side, reappear with DICKENSIAN CLERK, ALAN CLARE, DAZ

WARDEN, all talking at the same time — all exit prompt side except KAK and SHELTER MAN.

SHELTER MAN : I thought they'd never go.

KAK : Mummy was awfully upset about the bomb . . . she got radiation sickness, you know . . . privately, of course. . . . Daddy came in to me one morning, he said, 'Son', he knew that much. 'Mummy's got radiation sickness, she'll have to be put down . . .'

SHELTER MAN : Down where?

KAK : Down anywhere. . . .

SHELTER MAN : Ohh, there . . . some of my best friends are Jews, you know. . . .

KAK : When we got permission from the Ministry of Euthanasia we gave her a wonderful send-off . . . we let her wear Daddy's floral tennis frock . . . and took her to the Junior Carlton for tea . . . then we all went to see Son of Mousetrap. . . . The play's still running, you know. . . .

SHELTER MAN : But Agatha Christie's dead.

KAK : I'm sure she'd rather have it the other way round — well . . . Finally we took Mummy to the Young Conservatives Club for supper and choosing my moment I said, 'Mummy, the time clock on your pumps are undone.' She bent down to reset it and Father, timing his moment, passed her the bill and drew his sword . . . and (*overwrought*) I don't *have* to go on, do I???

SHELTER MAN: Unless it's a serial . . . of course you must go on.

KAK: Well, he plunged the sword into her back! When Daddy saw what he'd done, he put his head in the gas oven.

SHELTER MAN: That must have been terrible.

KAK: No, it was delicious! Well, it's getting dark . . .

SHELTER MAN: Still gets dark at night, does it?

KAK: Yes, old traditions die hard. . . .

Phone bells off.

KAK: The bells!

SHELTER MAN: Oh, you still have the telephone?

KAK: No, *only* the bells. . . .

Enter MATE with a green telephone, with the bell inside it ringing.

MATE: Are you the preferential Lux subscriber party wot's ordered the Daz party line phone?

KAK: Yes yes yes. . . .

MATE: No no no. This isn't it, sir, this is a model of the type you're going to get.

KAK: Let me answer that phone, the bells are driving me mad M A D mad.

MATE : Cat. C A T Cat.

KAK : Let me answer that Cat !

KAK closes with MATE and a terrific struggle ensues. All through the telephone bell rings. Fix working bell inside phone, button operated. The PIANIST starts to play loud, old-fashioned fight music. The SHELTER MAN moves around them like a referee. Finally, KAK rips phone from MATE.

KAK : Hello hello, Captain Pontius Kak here. What ? Who ? (*To MATE*) It's for you.

MATE : No no no no, I don't want to become an addict. I tell you in the hands of the wrong people that becomes a lethal weapon. For instance (*Picks up phone*) Hello ? Saigon, this is President Johnston, I haven't had my breakfast yet, so go and bomb a few villages. Napalm, yes. How ? Well done, I like 'em well done. (*Hangs up*) Or the Foreign Office. (*Posh*) 'Ello, Rhodesia ? Ah, Mr Smith ? Oh, this is the Hon Crappington Twoggle. Look, not a word to anyone, we're sending you some parcels of petrol, old boy, beat the old Sanctions, eh ? It'll all blow over — well, until then, get the Wogs to push 'em. (*Hangs up*) See ? Green telephones mean war !

SHELTER MAN : The only way to stop wars is to have them.

MATE : I better get orf to the library, burn a few more books. Not to mention Bazonka.

SHELTER MAN : Bazonka?

MATE : I keep telling you not to mention that! (*He goes mad*) Oooooh, Yaka-boo! (*Exits*)

SHELTER MAN : Where was he when the bomb dropped?

KAK : Right underneath it.

SHELTER MAN feels for invisible pocket of waistcoat, makes as though he has taken out a pocket watch.

SHELTER MAN : According to the lining of my waistcoat pocket, it's twenty to three.

KAK repeats the same pocket-watch routine as SHELTER MAN.

KAK : Then it's wrong. According to the lining of my pocket it's ten past four.

SHELTER MAN : But I put mine right by the lining of Big Ben. I must go, I left the gas on, she must be dead by now. Bye bye.

He leaps down the trap door, but bounces up again. This effect is done by putting a trampoline under the trap. He keeps bouncing up. Each time he comes up :

SHELTER MAN : Goodbye.

Let this get its quota of laughs, then KAK shoots him.

KAK : I had to. It could have gone on all night.

Phone rings. KAK answers it.

KAK: Hello? Just a minute!

Unzips his trousers, lowers them to his ankles. Picks up phone.

KAK: (*lovingly*) Hellllo, darling. What are you doing with yourself this evening? Oh, you can't do that alone, darling. Eh? When are we going to get married . . . not yet, darling, we're doing so well testing these contraceptives for W H I C H. . . . Yes, but the money's so good. Eh? How's the radiation up your way, eh? Oh, they're having it blessed by a priest. Well, keep taking the hormone tablets, it's bound to clear up. Eh, of course I do, you know, know I do. Bye bye, Geoffrey. (*Hangs up phone. Pats his legs*) Must get these legs lagged for the winter, must get some head lag as well. (*Hits his head*) It's no good, I must find my birth certificate. I had a packet of them somewhere. (*Feels in his waistcoat pockets*) Ah! Here we are. (*Puts it to his ear*) Good, it's still going. (*Looks at certificate*) 3rd April 1918! Gad, it's getting late, time for my Humiliation. (*Goes to hat stand*) Rubber Punishment Cap! (*He dons what appears to be a large sink pump with a flashing red light at the top of the handle*) Defeat of England Medal! (*Pins on a medal*) Piece of Hybrid Chalk. (*Takes chalk from pocket. Draws magic circle around himself. Braces himself. Switches on flashing light on Punishment Cap. Screams*) Nowwww.

Black out. Green pencil soft on KAK from above. B.P. screen silhouette of Britannia.

KAK: Ohhh, Your Majesty, Your Majesty, I'm sorry we lost the war, I'm sorry I failed you, I tried to catch the naughty bomb before it hit the Palace, but if you remember one of your corgis bit me and then . . .

Sound of the mule blowing raspberries. KAK goes into a frenzy of trying to beat the sound out of the air with a fly swat. Silhouette of Britannia also tries to do likewise. LITTLE MAN in leopard skin and club repeats his previous performance. Phone rings. All panic and sound stops. KAK rushes to phone, drops his trousers, speaks.

KAK: Hello, darling? Eh? (*Screams. Pulls up trousers. Holds them modestly with one hand*) Ohh, Lord Fortnum. I was just in training to phone you. What? It's happened? Didn't you take the pills? Give me the address. 29 Cul-de-Sac Place. I'll be right over. Keep taking the tablets.

Slams phone down. Claps his hands with a degree of joy. Picks up a suitcase from which the handle comes off in his hand, leaving case behind. Exits.
Pause. Sound off of PLASTIC MAC MAN: 'Arthur, Arthur, Arthur.' Enter PLASTIC MAC MAN. He wears black plastic mac, kinky boots, also a rubber punishment cap and red rubber sink gloves, carries a semi-inflated inner tube of a bicycle. He holds it crushed up. He leers at audience, secretively looks around in perverted manner to make sure he's alone. Gloats, throws inner tube on floor. Gloats, jumps into it, switches punishment light on cap. Looks at audience, suddenly whips open plastic mac, reveals he is wearing old woman's pink corset, whalebone

style, one long red stocking and one black. He prides himself on having done so. Starts to beat himself with tiny whip. Suddenly spot goes on, to reveal the feather bobbing on the psychiatric couch. Reacts. Rushes across to couch, lies on it, agitates feather.

PLASTIC MAC MAN: (*screams*) Arthurrrr, Arthur, Arthur!

Coffin lid flies up. MAN inside sits up.

COFFIN MAN: Shut up. There's people down here trying to get to sleep.

PLASTIC MAC MAN: Ahhhhhhhhhhhhhhhh.

CURTAIN

ACT TWO

Stage set:

Downstage right. Coffin.

Upstage right. Large double brass bed.

Upstage centre. Screen for changing behind.

Downstage centre. Table with two drawers with knobs. Two chairs.

Upstage left. Piano rostrum as Act One. At foot of piano, large silver salver with large cover (as at banquets).

Stage left. Chest of drawers with mirror. Oscilloscope disguised to look like a piece of furniture.

Spot on piano rostrum. At foot of PIANIST is large meat dish covered with salver. PIANIST plays an arpeggio. Raises lid of dish. Reveals head of a SINGER surrounded by food. He sings 'Whene'er I feel afraid'. End of song.

PIANIST covers SINGER with dish cover. Stage in half light to represent night-time. Enter PONTIUS KAK pushing a door. The door is portable and on wheels and LIGHT. *A small light is above the knocker. There is a small black plate on the door above the knocker, on which eventually KAK writes the number. He rings the bell on the door. Door opens. MATE in white nightshirt, nightcap and candle-holder with electric simulated candle which can be switched on and off on handle. FORTNUM's voice now comes over via mike as he is bedsitting room.*

MATE : Yers?

KAK : Is this Number 29 Cul-de-Sac Place?

MATE : No, mate, that's next door.

MATE closes door. KAK wheels door along to the right, leaving MATE standing like an idiot with a lighted candle.

MATE : Oh! (*Exits, blowing candle on and off*)

KAK stops door on prompt side. He writes number 29 *on the black plate.*

KAK : Ah, this must be the place. (*Rings the bell*) Hello? Hello? (*Rings*) Can you hear me? (*Rings*) I'm playing your tune.

FORTNUM : Go away, I'm not well. Who is it?

KAK : It's me, Dr Captain Pontius Kak, VC and Pin.

FORTNUM : Oh, come in, Captain Pontius Kak, PC and Vin.

KAK opens the door, enters and closes the door. The door moves across stage and exits opposite from side. This is done by one of the cast.

KAK: Ah hem. I've come about that piece of string they're auctioning at Sothebys.

FORTNUM: Thank God, I though you'd never get here. Now tell me, where am I?

KAK: Body Odour Mansions, 29A Cul-de-Sac Terrace.

FORTNUM: I know dat, that. But what borough?

KAK: It's pretty bad news, I'm afraid. It's Paddington.

FORTNUM: (*gasps and choking*) Quick, put a notice in that window. No coloured and no children and definitely no coloured children.

KAK: Don't worry. . . . Look, to avoid such possibilities, I'll tell you what I'm going to do—*I'll* move in with my knees and my fiancée, who is currently a virgin for a limited season.

FORTNUM: Harrods?

KAK: Yes, the Virgin Department. Now, I'd better run the old stethoscope over you.

He produces stethoscope from inside his jacket. MATE comes on with a door bell hung on his chest, and carrying a case and a cage with a rose growing inside. He now wears a BR porter's hat. He walks up to KAK and rings the bell on his chest.

KAK : Come in.

MATE : Ta. 'Ere, they're starting up Compulsory Happiness Classes again. And, oh yes, Billy Graham (*He crosses himself*) — he's going to have floodlit nude Bible reading at Wembley.

KAK : Thank heaven for that.

MATE : Thank you, heaven. 'Ere, let me help you with that heavy handle.

He indicates the handle of the suitcase that KAK is still carrying.

KAK : Put it up there. (*He points to suitcase*)

MATE : Yes, that's a good place. (*Looks at rose in cage*) Lovely rose — what's it called?

KAK : I call it Jim.

MATE : Oh, lovely — a rose called Jim. 'Ere, ha ha. (*Sly joke coming*) Why did the chicken cross the road?

KAK : I don't know, why did the chicken cross the road?

MATE : I don't know, I was asking you. Ha ha ha! Ha ha! (*Exits roaring with laughter. Re-enters still laughing*

KAK: Did you know that somebody, (*Takes MATE's hand and strokes it*) somewhere, needs you?

MATE: (*horrified*) Get him orft me. . . .

KAK: Come on, England's oldest consenting Male Adult.

MATE: Get 'im orft . . . Get. . . . Ohhh, unclean. . . . (*Exits*)

KAK: Thank heavens he's gone.

MATE re-enters in great scarlet coat from neck to ankles. The coat is made slit up the back, lined with satin for quick donning, and false front with buttons.

MATE: I haven't gone yet darling? (*Exits*)

KAK: Now, Lord Fortnum, let's have a look at you. (*Puts stethoscope on wall*) Breathe in.

Crosses to theatre wall. KAK breathes in. FORTNUM on mike breathes in. Lights dim quickly.

KAK: Out.

FORTNUM breathes out. Lights back to normal quickly.

KAK: (*opens trap door*) Say 'Ahhhh'.

FORTNUM: (*on mike*) Ahhhhhhh.

Puts stethoscope on table.

KAK : Now cough —

FORTNUM on mike coughs. Knob on drawer of table falls off. The table is a two-drawer table, with knobs on drawers. One knob can be displaced by pressing a fitment at the back of the table, which is done by CAPTAIN KAK.

KAK : Lord Fortnum, are you married?

FORTNUM : No.

KAK : Well, I should strongly advise against it.

Enter MATE in Boer War topee. He plays a bugle call on a life-sized stuffed turkey, a cornet being concealed inside.

KAK : It's all happening! London is a swinging town. (*He clicks his finger once*) One more timeeeeee! (*Clicks his finger again and hurts himself*)

MATE : Twit. It's the World War III Reunion Dinner. Food for other ranks, sir. . . . Champagne, dancing and sexual orgies for officers.

KAK : Din dins. . . . Don't wait up, Lord Fortnum, I'll be back at dawn. Like the Telly on?

FORTNUM : Yes, I'm mad for it, hear me, mad for it.

KAK : (*mounts the karzi with MATE*) Goodnight.

He holds up a long ceiling light switch on string. Pulls the string. Stage black out. From OP side a large television set on legs is moved on stage. Inside it are three men: BOB TODD, BILL KERR, JOHNNY VYVYAN. They are in the set visible from chest up, as in a medium long shot. Therefore they are dressed in evening dress from the waist up, below the screen level they are still in underwear. TODD wears ragged long underpants; BILL KERR wears ordinary boxer type underpants; JOHNNY VYVYAN wears a mini skirt, with white 'with it' stockings and high-heel shoes. The TV screen is illuminated from the inside with bright light bulbs not visible to the audience. These lights can be switched off from one of the knobs on side of the TV set.

BOB: Good evening. And I mean that most sincerely. This is BBC ONE AND ITV FIFTY SIX.

He puts on a dead-eye false smile.

BOB: It's ten o'clock and time for The News. I'm afraid at the moment there isn't any. The heavy radiation over England is still causing a black-out of all radio, TV and Telstar communications, but my milkman told me that England were all out for twenty-three, so Cowdrey declared. Now here to fill in the time is a talk on property by the Right Hon Cardinal Richard Crossman.

BILL: (*wearing spectacles. Full of false glib charm*) Good evening. I have just come from negotiating a successful sale of St Paul's Cathedral to Mr Onassis, who intends to pull it down and build a block of luxury self-contained St

Paul's Cathedralettes. There was a violent objection to this from John Betjeman, so we've sold him as well. A remarkable trend in the landlord business is the skyrocketing rents in Paddington since the discovery of people in them. Tiny one-room flatlets with twenty negroes in have been fetching a rent of fifty a week. (*Here BILL KERR goes on miming his talk*)

FORTNUM: Fifty pounds a week? Gad, this makes me a potential goldmine.

BILL: . . . that was no consenting male adult, that was my wife. Goodnight.

BOB: Good news, some news has just arrived via Telstar. Ahem. The effects of radioactive fallout are having strange mutation results: a Jamaican bus conductor in Highgate has turned into a ginger tom cat called Ned, several unconfirmed reports of people turning into birds should be taken with a certain degree of CLUCK CLUCK. I beg your parden, I'll read that bit again . . . should be taken with a certain degree of . . . (*Goes into a series of chicken clucks*)

He exits out of the TV set, through the slit black curtains at back of set.

SECOND ANNOUNCER: That is the end of television for this year. We'll be with you again next Boxing Day, when Charlton Heston will wrestle His Holiness the Pope for the Sportsman of the Year title. Till then, goodnight. (*Sings*) God

Save Mrs Gladys Scroake Long Live Mrs Gladys Scroake Long Live Gladys Scroake. Goodnight.

He reaches his hand out of the TV set and switches the set off. The lights in TV set go out. TV set moves off OP side quickly. Stage black out. Oscilloscope switched on from off stage.

FORTNUM: (*when he speaks, his speech vibrations light up oscilloscope*) Miss Hart?

Coffin lid shoots up, CORPSE sits up with typewriter in lap.

COFFIN MAN: Yes, sir?

FORTNUM: Take a letter. Dear Sir, Madam or consenting Male Adult, Prices of flats in Paddington rocketing fifty gns a week for one room like me. This illness will be an advantage. Signed Lord Fortnum.

During the dictation COFFIN MAN types like fury.

COFFIN MAN: Who shall I send it to?

FORTNUM: Me.

COFFIN MAN: Right.

He whips the paper out of the typewriter and the lid slams down on the coffin.

FORTNUM: Ha ha ha. I've become a man of

property, my condition must be valuable. Mmm, I wonder if I've got a large basement.

At this the light in the mirror frame of the chest of drawers comes on, showing a pale charlady's face: MRS GLADYS SCROAKE.

MRS SCROAKE: No, dear, you ain't got no basement.

FORTNUM: How do you know?

MRS SCROAKE: I bin down there, sir.

FORTNUM: How can you go down there if there isn't one? Wait a minute. Who are you? No, no, I'll rephrase that. How would you like to rent a room, fifty gns a week?

MRS SCROAKE: Wot? No thank you, I'm in enough trouble as it is. You know what happened to me last night?

FORTNUM: No.

MRS SCROAKE: Thank Gord fer that.

FORTNUM: You can tell me, madam, my mother was Godfrey Winn.

MRS SCROAKE: Well, it's this radiation, I've (*tearful*) I've turned into a Chest of Drawers.

The chest of drawers in question is an ordinary Victorian type, with a mirror on top. The mirror has been removed from the frame. Across it is stretched a transparent gauze, sprayed with a light silver paint. Behind the mirror small bulbs are placed so that when lit up, we can see through the gauze, the face of the person assuming the identity of the chest of drawers. The whole thing is on wheels, and must be very light and portable.

FORTNUM: My dear, how did this terrible thing happen?

MRS SCROAKE: Well, me and Mrs Gronk were scrubbing the steps of the Admiralty—

FORTNUM: So that's how it happened!

MRS SCROAKE: I haven't finished yet. Me and Mrs Gronk were doin' the steps when Boom, the Hatom bomb dropped, I got frighted when I see Charing Crost Station flyin' up in the air, Aida said you see, the trains will be runnin' late tonight. Just then, a railway carriage hit her on the head. 'Oh,' she said, 'I've come over all giddy.' I don't remember any more, I blacked out.

FORTNUM: A wise decision. You can recuperate in this charming flat at only fifty guineas a week.

MRS SCROAKE: . . . when I came to I remember I had changed into this chest of drawers, and I was in a second-hand furniture shop in the Harrow Road.

FORTNUM: Harrow? That's my old road.

MRS SCROAKE: Then this Pakistani seaman come in, he bought me for two nicker.

FORTNUM: Two knickers?

MRS SCROAKE: He took me to his flat, and used me to keep his chutney and curry in. (*Sobs*)

FORTNUM: There, there, your hot secret is safe with me, Mrs—Mrs . . .

MRS SCROAKE: Scroake, Gladys Scroake.

FORTNUM: Scroake? Aren't you the new Queen of England?

MRS SCROAKE: Yers.

FORTNUM: I'm pleased and honoured to meet you, Mrs Scroake Your Majesty.

MRS SCROAKE: Ta! Oh, I wish I could get home, my Arthur will be waitin' for 'is supper.

FORTNUM: Oh no, you must remain here, Your Majesty, you may be Arthur's wife, but you're on my inventory, to whit.

MRS SCROAKE: Who's a twit?

FORTNUM: No, you're part of my furnishings; you're all mine, possession is nine-tenths of the law, and three parts legal crap.

It is still black out. Enter PONTIUS KAK with a torch.

KAK : Lord Fortnum, Lord Fortnum, I'm back, I —

He shines torch up to the gallery.

KAK : No, he's not as tall as that. Click.

Stage lights up. Down stage OP side is portion of the wall of a room, wallpapered in a distinctive pattern. About eight feet high by about three to four feet wide. Very light in weight. Flown from above. Standing in front is MATE the traffic warden. Brown overall, flat cap. Bucket of wallpaper paste, paste brush, roll of wallpaper the same pattern as that on the wall. Seated at the table, mid stage, is a DELIVERY MAN. Brown overall, white plimsols, greasy trilby hat. Gray walrus moustache, iron frame spectacles. He holds two medium-sized framed oil paintings on his lap.

FORTNUM : Is that you, Kak?

KAK : Yes, and what a reunion — drinking, gallons of champagne, dancing naked on the tables, sexual orgies.

FORTNUM : Ohhhhh. Who else was there?

KAK : No one, just me. (*Suddenly sees the DELIVERY MAN*) Ohh.

DELIVERY MAN : Captain Kak, sir? Barkers

Delivery, sir. You ordered two Van Gogh paintings.

KAK : Ah yes, the Van Gogh. (*Sees MATE*) Who are you?

MATE : The van driver. Ha ha ha ha ha.

DELIVERY MAN : (*tapping his forehead with his finger*) He's training to be a twit, sir.

KAK : I see. Ahhh, hang this one up there.

He points to the wall with his finger.

DELIVERY MAN : Right, sir. (*He hangs painting on KAK's extended finger*)

KAK : On second thoughts, the wall.

DELIVERY MAN : Arthur, hang this on the wall.

KAK : Right, darlin'.

MATE hangs picture on wall. Quickly pastes a matching wallpaper over the Van Gogh (frame and all).

KAK : Beautiful : There's no doubt about it, Van Gogh was a great wallpaper.

He points to the second painting that the DELIVERY MAN is holding, which is a painting of a policeman.

KAK : Who painted that?

DELIVERY MAN : That's the other Van Gogh.

KAK : Nonsense, that's a Constable. Take it back.

DELIVERY MAN : Very well, sir. Come, Arthur.

As they exit, the wall is flown up. Hanging from the trailing edge are a pair of legs.

KAK : Lord Fortnum, I've decided to move into you.

FORTNUM : Oh.

KAK : I have my well-known fiancée, Miss Wilson, waiting outside in her Mini Minor Skirt.

FORTNUM : So?

KAK : What I'm trying to say is, she has nowhere to stay. I'm casting her on your mercy.

FORTNUM : Of course, for fifty guineas a week, she can have the room and the mercy thrown in free.

KAK takes out a cigarette case, from his pocket a ring of keys on a chain, he unlocks the case with a key, takes out a cigarette, lights it, puts it back into the case still alight. He does all this through the dialogue.

KAK : Lord Fortnum, as your psychiatrist I must strongly advise you against the taking of rent — it could aggravate your condition. I tell you bluntly . . . and I'll have to be sharp with you now . . . that *rent* once taken can have a terrifying hold on the victim — you could even develop into a condition known among the working class as . . . 'Bleedin' Landlord'.

FORTNUM : Oh, good heavens.

KAK : . . . you *must* control your rent. . . .

FORTNUM : Yes, yes, controlled rents . . . controlled strictly at fifty guineas a week. . . . (*Laughs madly*)

KAK : Lord Fortnum! (*He picks up chair and bangs it into stage*)

FORTNUM : Oh!

KAK : You see, your condition is far worse than you thought. I must move in before rent taking gets a hold on you.

FORTNUM : Very well, I'll put myself in your hands.

KAK : *When* I bring my financee in, I must ask you to remain silent and (*Intimately*) if you see anything that passes between people in love, well, try to control yourself.

Enter MISS PENELOPE WILSON, dressed by Mary Quant. She carries a parrot or a macaw on a perch (T shaped).

PENELOPE : Pontius.

KAK turns. Extends his arms to her.

KAK : Richard.

PENELOPE : It's Penelope.

KAK : Of course, Penelope, I didn't recognise you with your clothes on. Come, let me take your father.

He takes the perch.

KAK : Tsu tsu, the Right Honourable Harold Wilson, what a strange fate for a great statesman. Keep your pecker up, sir, could be worse, you could have turned into a Tory. (*Calls*) Boy?

Traffic Warden MATE enters.

MATE : (*laughingly*) Boy.

KAK : Boy.

KAK hands parrot to MATE.

MATE : I'll put him in Michael Foot's cage. Ha ha ha.

KAK turns to PENELOPE. Smiles.

PENELOPE : Darling, is the Vicar on his way?

KAK : Yes, on his way, full of love, a true Christian and a Major Share holder in ICI.

PENELOPE: Then I'll just go and slip into an old wedding dress.

She strips off her dress in one go.

FORTNUM: (*great wolf whistle*) Corrrrrrr.

KAK: No, no, Penelope. Er—behind the screen.

PENELOPE: Darling, you've seen me undressed before.

KAK: All right, I'll come behind the screen with you then.

Both behind the screen. KAK reappears with a list and pencil. PENELOPE undresses and throws her things over the top of screen. As they appear, KAK ticks them off. To each one he names the items in military jargon.

KAK: Slupps, nylon, one. Knickers, black, silk, one. Brassiere, bosoms, for the covering of, one.

A skeleton is thrown over the top of screen.

KAK: No need to go that far, darling.

Sound off of a VICAR approaching, chanting a hymn. He appears prompt side pushing a barrow, mounted with a baroque portable altar with candles, angels, the lot. NB —Built into the centre of the altar is a till, disguised to look like part of altar. VICAR is dressed in red and white hooped striped knee-length bathing costume, clerical collar and black attachment, pince-nez on black ribbon, frog mask, black below-the-knee socks with white broad elastic band tops to match his clerical collar.

VICAR: Weddings, get your lovely weddings here, baptisms, cut-price confirmations done while you wait. Weddings, instant weddings.

KAK: Ahhhh, Vicar. I wrote to you, I'm Pontius.

VICAR: Not Pilate?

KAK: No, I'm not a pilot, I'm a captain. We'd like a quick wedding before lunch.

VICAR: Of course you won't stop for that. Now — um — may I offer you the new economical combined wedding and divorce, three pounds ten and you get custody of the wedding cake.

KAK: Sorry, I can't afford a divorce at the moment, I think it might upset her. Of course, later on when I'm earning, I'll go for the full annulment. Oh, the frog mask.

VICAR: Oh, you've noticed. I specialise in underwater weddings, I'm the only one, you know. I did Hans and Lotte Hass. Now, is your instant bride ready?

KAK: Penelope?

PENELOPE runs on in a transparent knee-length black nightie, a bridal veil.

PENELOPE: I'm ready, darling.

VICAR: (*leering over the bride*) Hello, my dear. . . . (*To KAK*) I must have some of the wedding photographs, there's bound to be transparencies, joke, ha ha ha. Now, as a special favour I'm going to give you the king-size wedding with the flip top Bible. . . . (*Holds up Bible*) Man, you are never alone with one of these. . . . Now, will you both hold hands, please. (*KAK clasps his own hands and PENELOPE clasps her own hands*) Good, good . . . now then. (*Opens book and starts intoning*) And, the naughty gamekeeper took her into the potting shed and laid her on the ground (*Starts to get excited*) . . . then with hands trembling he *ripped the thin silk* . . .

KAK: I say, look here. . . . That's not the Bible. . . . That's *Lady Chatterley's Lover.*

VICAR: Yes, I know, but it's packing them in the church every Sunday. However, if you prefer the old twit ceremony I think I still recall it. . . . Now then . . . (*Intones*) Do you Captain Pontius Kak take this bust 38 hips 36 to be your lawfully wedded wife?

KAK: (*intones back*) I was expecting you to ask me that . . . and it just so happens that I do. . . .

VICAR: (*intones*) Good, good, good. . . . (*Changes key*) Do you Penny-lope Wilson take this lawfully wedded sex maniac to be your husband?

PENELOPE : (*intones*) I do.

VICAR : Oh dear . . . that puts me out of the running. . . . (*Changes key*) Do you Penny-lope Wilson the well-known fiancée and bunny club hostesss promise to cherish your consenting male adult husband . . . to love, honour and obey him in sickness and in health, in trial and ordeal until death do you part and all that jazz? (*During this speech KAK undresses; he has a suit of pyjamas on under his uniform*)

PENELOPE : (*intones*) I do.

VICAR : (*intones*) You must be out of your mind. . . .

KAK : Look here, damn you ! There's *still* some decency left ! Come on, darling ! Let's go to bed ! ! ! !

VICAR : I haven't finished yet. I now pronounce you man and wife. . . .

KAK hands money to VICAR, who presses a lever on his portable altar — out shoots the drawer of a concealed till — puts money in. VICAR takes starting pistol. MAN with checkered car racing flag enters OP.

VICAR : On your mark . . . set. . . . (*Fires pistol*)

KAK and PENELOPE race for the bed and jump in. Confetti from flies. Sound of grand organ playing Wedding March. Peal of wedding bells. KAK picks up loud hailer, shouts.

KAK: Get out of my bedroom, you Peeping Tom.

All the bells and the organ are now faded out as VICAR exits. He trundles his barrow off.

VICAR: Get your holy bargains here, holy bargains week for fifty-two weeks only. Green Shield Stamps with every barmitzva. Die on your wedding day and get two ceremonies for the price of one. Pins stuck in clay models of your bank manager.

He pushes his barrow into wings, in exchange is handed a straw hat and cane. PIANIST plays a razz ma tazz intro. VICAR, leering, sings.

VICAR: Thank heaven for little girlsssssss.

A hook comes out of wings and pulls him off.

PENELOPE: Darling, we're alone at last.

KAK: Yes, what shall we do? I know — I spy with my little eye, something beginning with—

MATE pops up from behind bed. He has a divining twig in his hands.

MATE: Gladys? Gladys? Where are you, I want my supper, Glad. . . . I — oh, sorry, I'm looking for my missus.

KAK: Well, this one's mine. I've got the receipt.

The BRIDE and GROOM cuddle down in bed. MATE stands looking at them. Then goes over to the coffin. Sits down. And just looks at the audience.

MATE: It's orrl rite, we ain't forgotten the words. This is the bit the Lord Chamberlain cut, and I'm the twit trying to fill in the time. 'Ere's a limerick I heard . . .

VICAR puts head around wings.

VICAR: (*sings*) Ahhhhhhhhmennnnnnn.

MATE dives into the wings. Reappears swinging a life-size soft dummy dressed like the VICAR, which he hurls across the stage.

MATE: Well, that put the fear of God up 'im. Now where's Gladys, Glad . . . Glad. . . .

GLADYS: (*from behind chest of drawers or from wings*) 'Ere I am, Arthur. . . .

MATE: Oh, darlin', what 'ave they done to you. . . . Don't be ashamed, I know what happened . . . don't be ashamed. . . . I got the newspaper cutting here from the *News of the World*. . . . Quote. . . . Indian seaman . . . strange conduct in London doorway with second-hand chest of drawers. . . . I didn't know the chest of drawers was married, he tells Paddington Judge. . . . Abdul Raman Rates Jajiboo, Indian wog seaman of no fixed trousers, was accused at Paddington Assizes of indecent conduct. When questioned by the constable he said . . . I just had two beers and a small Bombay curry and I wasn't feeling very well. Everything went black . . . laughter in court. . . . He said he was a seaman smuggling monkeys to the RSPCA. He claimed he was sailing from Glasgow to Madras but unexpectedly ended up at Elba. He accused the ship's captain of not knowing his Madras from his . . .

GLADYS : Come on, Arthur, I want to go 'ome.

ARTHUR : Orl rite — orl rite. . . . I daren't tell her . . . I been unfaithful, I been goin' out wiv an airing cupboard, ha ha ha ha.

He exits with chest of drawers. Enter man dressed as a DIPLOMAT. Black Anthony Eden hat, black jacket, striped City trousers, black shoes. He holds a dispatch case with the Royal Cypher on flap. He is seated on a water closet on wheels, above him is the cistern, a chain and a handle. A CD plate is visible on side of cistern. From out of the cistern is the end of a tiger's tail. He is pushed by a small man made up like Quasimodo, with an exaggerated hump in his back, but wearing a CHAUFFEUR's hat. DIPLOMAT makes noise of a motor car and pretends to steer.

DIPLOMAT : Brrrrrrr. Parp parp. Stop here! Call back for me in ten minutes, I've got some unfinished business to attend to.

CHAUFFEUR : Right, sir.

He exits making motor-car noises.

DIPLOMAT : Ting a ling a ling. Buzzzz buzzzzz, knock knock knockity knick.

KAK : Who is it?

DIPLOMAT : Coitus Interruptus.

KAK : You swine, I've a good mind to kill you.

DIPLOMAT : Don't come too close, I've got Diplomatic Immunity. Allow me to introduce myself. Carlton Towers. Foreign Secretary.

KAK : Oh.

DIPLOMAT : I have urgent dispatches for the Prime Monster. The Hon. Wilson.

KAK : I'll go and get him. Excuse the mess, but we got the Socialists in.

He exits as he talks on prompt side.

DIPLOMAT : Penelope! What are you, my wife, doing in bed with another man?

PENELOPE : Carlton, I'm sorry, I've married again. I thought you were dead. I waited for you to return, you did leave me.

DIPLOMAT : Yes, but that was only this morning, to go to work.

PENELOPE : Was I impatient?

Re-enter KAK carrying the parrot on his perch.

KAK : Here he is, all merry and bright.

DIPLOMAT : We'd like to be alone — confidential stuff, you understand. (*As he speaks he sets the parrot's perch in a hole in the table, then undoes the diplomatic bag. DIPLOMAT looks closely at the parrot's face*) Sorry to see you like this, sir, I hope you're back to normal before the next election. Oh, Mr Michael Foot asked me to give you this. It's Sage Stuffing. (*He opens a small packet preferably with parrot food in so the parrot will eat*) Mr Brown is carrying on as Deputy Leader as best as he can, not as easy for him as a cocker spaniel. Mrs Wilson is well and is arranging for you to see the Curator of Birds at the Zoo, she says he may be able to help your present condition. The deposed Kabaka of Buganda has called the natives of Paddington to arms and declared Paddington an independent State, and is calling for free elections. Mr Smith has sent a telegram sympathising with us and wants to know if he can help. There's nothing else, sir, still no news as to who won the war. The Americans are still bombing Vietnam and Alabama. . . . Soho has been declared a wildlife reserve, Harry Secombe has become a nudist colony, and oh I see you've tabled a motion, sir. Goodbye, sir, and remember, sir, happiness is Egg shaped.

He places all spare props, clothes, etc, on the table, goes off doing train noises. He exits only to return with a SOLDIER in his arms. The SOLDIER's uniform and make-up are divided in half. His left side is a brigadier with red tabs, riding boot, red band round cap; his face is an old colonel's, white cavalry moustache. The other half is of a young sergeant, with a black moustache, World War One puttee, one black boot.

BRIGADIER: Put me down, put me down, man. Haven't you read the Highway Code?

DIPLOMAT: No, I'm waiting till they make the film.

A tent flies down. NB—This is only a mock-up. Just need the front of a tent, with an in-and-out flap to come through. The tent falls in front of the BRIGADIER. He pops his head through tent flap.

BRIGADIER: What a lovely day for a war—and Sergeant?

SERGEANT: Sah?

BRIGADIER: Hurry up, damn you.

SERGEANT: (*salutes*) Just callin' I'm sah. (*Walks to KAK. Does impression of a bugle call*) Compliments of the season, sir, Brigadier Fumbling Grope would like very much to see you, sir. Sah.

KAK leaps up.

KAK: Gad, duty calls. (*He feels under pillow, puts on a steel helmet painted to match his striped pyjamas. Next scene very Noël Coward*) Goodbye Dolly, I must leave you.

PENELOPE : We don't want to lose you but we think you ought to go.

KAK : Let me like a soldier fall.

PENELOPE : Land of Hope and Glory, mother to the free.

KAK : Keep the home fires burning. And, darling, if I shouldn't come back, I want you to give this to your mother. (*Hands her something*)

PENELOPE : Your cheque book.

KAK : She always wanted it.

PENELOPE : Darling, I'll get it to her if I have to cash every cheque myself.

KAK quick march. Sound effect: Cheers of crowd as soldiers march by to a brass band playing some patriotic march. KAK and SERGEANT march madly to BRIGADIER's tent. SERGEANT turns to show BRIGADIER face.

BRIGADIER : Pontius.

KAK : Philip.

BRIGADIER : Terence.

KAK : Rupert.

BRIGADIER : Bourne.

KAK : Hollingworth.

BRIGADIER : Fortnum.

KAK : And Mason.

BRIGADIER : Derry and . . .

KAK : Dick.

During the above KAK and BRIGADIER go through insane handshaking that eventually gets them tangled like all-in wrestlers.

BRIGADIER : Now then, who the hell are you?

KAK : Captain Kak, Third Foot, Seventh Teeth and the Ninth Symphony.

BRIGADIER : What proof?

KAK : Jeeves!

Enter DUSTMAN with a wheelbarrow loaded with old tins, forks and any lightweight resonant rubbish.

KAK : Show the Brigadier my credentials.

DUSTMAN tips rubbish on stage.

BRIGADIER : That's good enough for me. Now, you know why I've called you here.

KAK : No.

BRIGADIER: Oh, never mind, I'll think of something. Ah, War Office have had numerous requests for a return visit of World War One.

KAK: (*beaming*) Sir, I knew we hadn't heard the last of that old favourite. I remember the number of times my father used to sing me to sleep with it.

Black out. Spot on OLD SOLDIER in long trench coat, World War One overcoat, smothered in mud, ragged, on OP side. OLD SOLDIER takes what looks like a stick grenade from his belt. It is in fact a hand mike.

OLD SOLDIER: (*sings*) Bang bang boom. (*Does impression of machine guns, etc etc*) Let me like a soldier fall.

BRIGADIER draws his revolver and shoots him. KAK holds up a Juke Box Jury hit disc.

KAK: Oh, they don't write wars like that any more. I vote it a hit.

BRIGADIER holds up his disc with 'Hit'. A MAN leaps on from prompt side dressed as a housewife with a disc 'Mrs'. Exits embarrassed.

BRIGADIER: Good, then you'll help bring it all back. We'll have no difficulty finding backers for it, Krupps, Vickers Armstrongs, Skoda, all reliable people — where would wars be without them?

KAK: (*points to floor*) Over there.

Both step rapidly to the spot.

BRIGADIER : Correct. Now, there's a difficulty. Since World War One, travelling expenses have rocketed. Neither side can afford a war any more.

KAK : Tsu Oh.

BRIGADIER : Ah, but — a compromise. Rather than lose this golden opportunity, both sides have agreed to kill, maim and wound their own soldiers.

During the conversation, BRIGADIER takes out a leather cheroot case, opens it, hands it to KAK. From it KAK takes a white plastic clothes peg (large size) which he clips to his steel helmet. As does the BRIGADIER.

BRIGADIER : Just think, you can be killed in the privacy of your own home, free of charge. Picture the scene : Saturday afternoon, Private Tommy Atkins, his wife and his kids gathered round the telly watching Emergency Ward Ten eleven and twelve. Suddenly a friendly knock on the door, enter RSM Warrington, with a 'Hello, Tommy, it's your turn', bang bang, down he goes, happily clutching his sword, and before he's even cold, Mrs Atkins is getting the pension and living happily with the RSM.

KAK : It sounds too good to be true. How much happier World War One could have been. When, sir, where, how?

BRIGADIER : Now where do you want to serve?

KAK : Front line, sir.

BRIGADIER : (*looking at his list*) That'll be the Oliver Messel Suite at the Dorchester.

KAK : Oh, that means Peter Sellers will have to move.

BRIGADIER : (*calls*) Orderly!

ORDERLY comes carrying stretcher out of tent.

ORDERLY : Kitchener needs you! (*He has Kitchener moustache, is wearing long woollen combs, Army hat, Red Cross armband, and has an over-sized rubber finger over his own*)

ORDERLY/FIELD-MARSHAL : Well, he certainly doesn't need you. Five-four-three-two-one.

Tent flies out at speed. Sound of rocket.

BRIGADIER : Yes. Now where's me catalogue of wounds?

He refers to a small book.

BRIGADIER : Ah, Front Row. Ah here, you're lucky — there's only three vacant wounds on that row. How do you fancy this. . . . Orderly! (*ORDERLY attention*) Bullet in tibia, steel fragment in lung. (*The ORDERLY clutches the two parts*) Well?

KAK: No, no, I don't like that — not heroic enough for an officer.

BRIGADIER : Orderly ! Bayonet wound in buttock, sword hack at throat, shrapnel in the colonic.

ORDERLY takes on aspect of wounds. Eyes crossed, tongue out.

KAK : Noooo, no, looks too funny.

BRIGADIER : I know what you want. Dignity, simplicity, eh ? Orderly ! Bullet wound in temple. Mind you, it's fatal, but with a posthumous VC.

KAK : (*excited*) May I try ?

He takes up the pose.

KAK : (*calls*) Penelope ! Wait till she sees that. . . .

PENELOPE : Oh, darling . . . is it . . .

KAK : Fatal. It was the Rage of Flanders.

PENELOPE : Then it's you, Pontius.

She dons a widow's black veil. KAK lies in state on the stretcher.

There is a stage trick I want to try here. It means cutting the stage floor into a length the size of a man lying down. The piece is then fitted with an axle at each end and put back into the stage in its original level, except now it can be revolved. If we fix the underside with bolts so that should anyone stand on it, from above, it will not move. But if KAK lies down on that piece, he can be screened from the audience by a blanket being prepared to cover him, then the bolts underneath can be undone. The piece of wood can be revolved so that KAK slides into the floor, then put upright, leaving the space clear, KAK having miraculously vanished. I should like the Props Department to approach me about this as soon as possible. From the wings a MOURNER with black crêpe top hat and wreath appears. As does the traffic warden (MATE) with black band on his arm. The lid of coffin shoots up. Green light from within. Stage black out.

CORPSE: It's a bloody awful life being dead.

OMNES: Screwed down inside a coffin lined with lead.

Song 'Being Dead', Milligan, Edgington.

CURTAIN

INTERVAL SKETCHES (1)

House tabs taken up about three feet. Legs seen running about as though tabs had jammed. Some effort made to raise tabs by hand. ACTOR in dressing-gown eventually ducks underneath tabs.

ACTOR: Good evening. I've just come here to tell you that this is the self-same interval that they used in *Treasure Island* which has been brought back by popular request. I should also like to take the opportunity to thank Mrs Herbert J. Quirk of Battersea; it's not that we have anything to thank her for, it's just that she's *never* been thanked for anything in her life and we thought she might like it.

Now the next part of this show is unfit for the ears of children. If you have any children's ears on you, would you please put them in a box and hand them in to the attendant.

And now, for a certain kind of entertainment. (*Off: Loud agonised female screams*) Coming, dear!

He exits through tabs, revealing the back of his immaculate silk dressing-gown in rags revealing even tattier and ragged underwear, long underpants with low seat.

INTERVAL SKETCHES (2)

KAK and SWANEE WHISTLE PLAYER come in front of tabs. KAK sets up music stand for WHISTLER. WHISTLER hands KAK copy of music which turns out to be 'Private Eye'. KAK places 'Private Eye' on music stand and sings 'My Blue Heaven' (can be any music really), with WHISTLER following him. Yellow pole appears with parcel on end borne by MATE and DELIVERY MAN. (This towards end of song.)

MATE: Put it down there, where the parcel is.

DELIVERY MAN : You are the officer wot was in charge of the British deterrent in the last atomic war?

KAK : Yes, I was responsible for the delivery of it. I'd like to have seen those Ruskies' faces when it arrived.

DELIVERY MAN : Bad news, it has been returned to sender. (*Exit WHISTLER in panic*)

MATE : And there's ninepence to pay on it, mate.

KAK : What! I had that bomb dispatched to Moscow the moment we got imminent warning red. Ah, those Ruskies didn't think we had the means of delivering the bomb . . . they overlooked the fact that we have the finest postal system in the world.

DELIVERY MAN : To think, sir, that bomb cost us five hundred million pounds.

MATE : And still ninepence to pay, sir. Insufficient stamps.

KAK : We had to economise somewhere. . . . Put it in the fridge. . . . (*Tabs open to disclose Act II*) Keep it fresh. . . . There's always the Chinese.

MATE : There's seven hundred million of them.

KAK : They've only got themselves to blame. (*As DELIVERY MAN and MATE exit*)

ACT THREE

THE TIME : *Christmas Eve, 1979.*
NB — In this scene everyone is thinner, whiter and raggeder.

Set on stage as follows:
Piano rostrum is moved centre up stage.
Set large iron roller mangle upstage left.
Baby's cot (rocking type Moses basket or old-fashioned wooden rocker).
Wicker washing basket downstage left. Rose in flower pot, inside birdcage, is set anywhere on small round single-stem support, three-legged Georgian table.
A small long-nozzle white watering can.
Flown from above is a long washing line, all babies' nappies save THREE *babies' socks.*
Brass double bedstead in same position as before.
Table and two chairs centre stage.
In drawer of table are carving knife, two ordinary knives, two forks, two white enamel tea mugs.
An ordinary rubber deck quoit.
One rubber-topped xylophone mallet.
A large metal xylophone note (middle C), mounted in a small cradle, so that when struck it can vibrate.
One green van guard's flag.
A round portable oil stove with a light inside to simulate it is on.

CAPTAIN KAK is reading a newspaper that appears to be 'The Times' save its title : 'The Times Daily Worker'. PENELOPE is fussing about, improvising housework. She is wearing black, with a black woollen jumper. KAK is wearing a thick scarf and woollen gloves. KAK bangs his hands to get warm.

KAK : Good heavens, it's nearly three years since the war. Times flies. . . . Investigations are still going on as to find out who won. At the United Nations the British delegate suggested they draw lots for it. (*Turns the page*) Darling, listen to this. 'A barbeque. On Sunday the Mayor of Hampstead will set fire to the last mound of war corpses on the Heath. This will conclude the Government's two-year burial plan.' You see, things *are* getting back to normal.

FORTNUM : They're not back to normal. What about me? (*KAK tries to shhh him down*) Three years I've been like this. You haven't paid any rent, you haven't even had me redecorated, and on top of that you and your wife have had two children.

KAK : Well, we ate one, didn't we?

FORTNUM : Yes, you bloody cannibal! (*KAK leaps up*)

KAK : How dare you call nourishment cannibalism? We've got to eat, haven't we? We've got to survive. We can't go on living on grass and rats. They're all eating their children, there's nothing else. We're unlucky, we only had two. Most women are having litters of ten and twelve — the more kids we have the better fed we are. We've got to survive, haven't we? In early days if we hadn't eaten our dead we'd have all died. In any case the Minister of Food has legalised it. Do you know what they had for the Lord Mayor's Banquet this year?

FORTNUM: What?

KAK: Lord Boothby. Fricassee of Boothby. They said he was lovely. No, we've got to carry on as though nothing happened, decently, back to our more normal standards.

Enter PENELOPE carrying silver salver with domed cover.

PENELOPE: Dinner's ready, darling.

KAK: And what have we got today, rats?

PENELOPE: No. Surprise!

KAK lifts lid off, sees a slip of paper on dish, reads it.

KAK: Face north. (*He does so*) Take five paces forward. (*He does so*) Look under bed?????

PENELOPE nods her head. KAK gropes under bed. Voice under bed: 'Owwwww.'

KAK: Sorry. Ah. (*He takes out a whole roast chicken*) Oh, din dins, mmmmmmm. (*Sharpens knife*) What is it, chicken?

PENELOPE : No, it's Daddy.

KAK : Never mind, dear, we can let his perch to another bird.

He goes to carve.

PENELOPE : Be gentle, Pontius.

KAK : Don't worry, darling. I'll cut him on his right wing. Ha, ha, ha, ha. (*Sees PENELOPE staring at him*) Tell me, how did this *terrible* thing happen?

PENELOPE : He was asked to resign as Prime Minister, so he threw himself off his perch. He left this note on the piano.

The xylophone note mounted on a cradle is swung from the wings on thin black thread into the waiting hand of PENELOPE. She hands it to KAK, who places it on the table and hits it with the rubber-topped xylophone mallet.

KAK : A Flat? God, he must have suffered.

Enter MATE the traffic warden, carrying a red danger lamp. He has a balaclava on and an extra scarf.

MATE : Look what some idiot left on top of a pile of rocks, right in the middle of the road —

He is interrupted by the scream of car brakes, then a great crash as a car goes through a shop window.

MATE: Good job I brought this in, it would have broken to bits. (*Bangs his hands. Sees chicken*) Gor, food. What have we got here, then?

KAK: (*aside so as to shield PENELOPE*) It's Mr Wilson.

MATE: Oh, this will mean an election (or by-election).

Both KAK and MATE laugh and take a leg each. As they go to eat PENELOPE prays.

PENELOPE: Bless us, O Lord, and these Thy gifts which we are about to receive through Jesus Christ our Lord.

KAK: (*falsely*) Amen. (*Nudges MATE*)

MATE: Yer. Amen. Doesn't she know God's dead?

KAK: I didn't have the heart to tell her.

MATE: Harold, this is your finest hour, mate. (*Eats the leg*) Minister of Daz and Statistics says the population of England now stands at 950.

KAK: Soon have enough for another war.

MATE: War? That's all you bloody upper class ever think of. You all love war. You haven't got the guts to say so, 'cause you know it's wrong, so what does the Warrior Class do to hide its conscience? It invents a thing called Preservation of Peace. To have that Preservation, you got to have an army, and when you got an army you got to have a war, and what's the war for? The Preservation of Peace. And not only that, you worship heroes. It's thanks to heroes we got wars. Sod the heroes! Let's all be lovely kind cowards and live in peace.

KAK: Look, you working-class Daz Area people don't understand. War brings out the best in people.

MATE: Look, you saying we got to start killing each other to say how much we love each other? Wallop. I think you're a nice chap. Wallop. I like you too. Ahh, your class loves war. And all the glory. One minute you're a bank manager, next you're a captain with a batman, staff car, Officers' Mess. . . . You love it.

KAK: We do not. Don't you try to tell me I like wars. I'm just as fond of peace as you are.

MATE: No you're not, mate. You're war-loving bastards. All you Lux people are.

KAK: (*leaps up, grabs carving knife*) Look, I'm warning you, I do want peace.

MATE: No you don't!

KAK: (*fury*) I'm a peace-loving man. *I tell you I love peace!!* (*Raises knife*)

PENELOPE : (*reappears*) What are you fighting about?

MATE : Peace.

PENELOPE : Come on, eat your dinner before the radiation gets it.

Sound of air-raid sirens. Lights on stage dim to a greeny and amber mixture to make it look depressing.

MATE : 'Ere, that's Atomic Fog Warning, Grade A.

VOICE OVER P.A. : Radiation! Take cover. Masks on!

KAK, MATE and PENELOPE put on false bulbous 'Charlie Caroli' red noses, with small black toothbrush moustache underneath, and thick black 'George Robey' type eyebrows.

MATE : Oh, just in time. My word, it come down quick tonight. One whiff of this stuff and you've had it.

KAK : It's a good thing the Minister of Defence had a sense of humour when he introduced these. After all, the old-fashioned gas mask hid the dignity of the human face.

MATE : Yes, yes, it makes a difference. Well, I don't think the human face meets the modern need.

KAK is eating all through this. PENELOPE comes on with a teapot.

PENELOPE : (*to MATE*) Tea or coffee?

MATE : Tea.

She pours tea into his mug. Looks at KAK.

KAK : Coffee.

PENELOPE pours from same pot into his mug.

MATE : This is 'ot water.

KAK : Yes, but well, we've got to keep up the . . . We mustn't lose our dignity, we must improvise. . . .

MATE : I was saying, in the hurly-burly of post-Atomic living, I'd put a bloke's mouth on top of his nut.

KAK : Why?

MATE : Why? Well, then, when he's late for work he can put his breakfast under 'is 'at, and eat it on the way to the orfice.

KAK : Jolly good. Jolly good.

The lights go a little dimmer. Silence. Fade up the sound of a ticking clock. A very heavy steady hall clock type of tick.

MATE : (*for the first time deadly serious*) I wonder what's going to become of us all.

KAK : Eh? Well, we'll just have to keep going.

MATE : What for?

KAK : Because we're British.

MATE : British? Standing army, three. Members of Parliament, four. Doctors and teachers, nil. Population eight hundred and seventy-four, seven hundred of 'em with radiation sickness. We're all doomed, mate. No proper grub. I'm covered in these sores. There's no hope . . . Man is finished. And we asked for it.

KAK : Nonsense. When the Conservatives get in again things will be all right, eh, darling?

He looks across at PENELOPE, who has just gone to the baby's cradle with a bottle of milk. She has tested it for heat on the back of her hand. She goes to put it into the cot.

PENELOPE : (*screams*)

KAK : Penelope, wh —

PENELOPE : He's dead, my baby's dead. Robin — Robin — Robin! (*She collapses sobbing onto the cradle*)

MATE : She forgot his gas mask.

KAK : But she didn't forget his name.

Silence. Distant mournful sound of ship's hooter (like 'Queen Mary's'). Distant sound of Big Ben striking the quarter. MATE takes out his watch. Looks at it.

MATE : You — you better go and chat her up.

KAK : (*nods. Puts on a smile*) Cheer up, darling. (*He crosses to her*) We can always have another one, now we've discovered what causes them. (*To MATE*) Can't we, *chum*?

MATE : Yerss. Cheer up, darlin', no need to let that milk go to waste. I'll drink that for you. (*Takes bottle, starts to drink*)

KAK : Look. Look. Look, he's got the hang of it, just like Robin. Look, why don't we adopt him? (*KAK thrusts baby's rattle into PENELOPE's hand, then holds her wrist and shakes rattle at MATE*) Dibbum, dubbium, does Dibbiums like his bot-bot?

MATE : (*shaking bottle*) 'Ere, this bleedin' stuff won't come out.

KAK : Darling, his first words. . . . (*He tries to shake PENELOPE out of her gloom. He suddenly grabs MATE's arm and walks him briskly downstage*) Something's upset her tonight, must be Robin. He was our first child, or rather first monster, and she's going to miss him. Still, it means meat on Sunday.

MATE : Me and Her Majesty, Mrs Scroake, got a kid. Don't know what we'd do without 'im. He's too thin to eat. When I get home at night, there he is, crawling all over the floor with his nappies round his ankles. I am a bit worried about him.

KAK : Oh, why?

MATE : He's forty-two!

KAK : That's a good age for a child.

MATE : (It's a good age for that gag, too!)

KAK : (*calls to PENELOPE cheerfully*) Come on, poppet. I'll tell you what . . . let's open that last bottle of Flag Sauce and count our knees.

MATE : That's a good game.

Both pull trousers up around knees. Wife stands up.

PENELOPE : Knees! Knees! That's all you ever think about. . . . Night after night it comes . . . let's count our knees . . . and what do we get . . . every night the same total . . . two each.

Lights full up.

KAK : You must be patient, darling. In these times we have got to make our own entertainment.

PENELOPE gives basket to KAK and starts gathering nappies from line.

PENELOPE : I carried little Robin inside me for eighteen months rather than let him out into this world.

KAK : Now, come on, darling. . . . We're only human . . . well, *we* are. . . . Robin . . . he was just a thing.

They arrive at the THREE *socks on line.*

PENELOPE : He was *our* thing . . . it was my own precious baby . . . it was the only thing I cared for in this filthy, insane, dying, stinking civilisation.

KAK : I put his name down for Geelong Grammar School and, just in case, Roedean. What more can a man do!

Fog siren hoot. Dismal silence.

MATE : (*burps*) 'Ere, where are you two going for your summer holidays?

KAK : *Harrods,* of course.

MATE : Which department?

KAK : Sportswear and Sun Lamps this year. . . .

MATE : You've got a few bob.

KAK : Got a bit salted away.

PENELOPE : They've got nice plastic grass at

Harrods. Robin used to play on it. . . . (*Breaks down*) Oh!

MATE: I can't afford your class. Me and my missus has to be satisfied with a week under a sun lamp at the Co-op.

KAK: That's a good working man's resort . . . might even call it a last resort. (*Bursts into loud guffaws*)

MATE: Hear that funny joke your old man made? Talkin' of grass, I was walkin' through Hyde Park this mornin' and the workmen were paintin' all the trees black for the winter . . . and, oh yes, they were gettin' all the plastic snowdrops ready for the spring. They looked lovely . . . yes. . . . O' course, they'll never be as good as real snowdrops. Still, they're better than nothin'. You know, it beats me, these scientists, they split the atom, they got to the moon, they destroyed civilisation, and none of the clever bastards knew how to make a snowdrop. That's what they called Scientific Progress. Ha, ha, ha, ha, ha, ha.

The lights on the stage light up. A bell sounds off stage.

VOICE ON P.A.: All clear. All clear.

Enter a SEA CAPTAIN in Mediterranean white uniform. Immaculate. The nappies are flown. Behind the SEA CAPTAIN comes a portable ship's steering wheel with ship's telegraph with bells inside. A SEAMAN in Ordinary Seaman's uniform pushes it on. Sound of seagulls and washing of the sea.

CAPTAIN: All passengers ashore. Full speed ahead, MacGregor.

SEAMAN: Aye aye, sir.

CAPTAIN: Hoist the spikkion and targle the blundion.

Voice in wings answers all the calls in the seafaring method of hailing.

Immediately KAK starts playing deck quoits with PENELOPE. MATE wraps a BLANKET *around his knees and dons* DARK GLASSES.

SEAMAN: Will you take your partners for the Extermination Waltz.

Sound of tinny gramophone record of 1925 one-step. KAK dances with PENELOPE. The CAPTAIN dances with MATE. All stand-ins come on dressed in the most garish costumes they can manage.

CAPTAIN: Are you enjoying the trip, Madame?

MATE: (*imitating a woman, a refined woman*) Hoh no, Hi ham hused to a much higher klarss of vessel. I mean, in the brokure, it says sunshine tours. I've hain't seen the bleedin' sun since we left Hingland.

CAPTAIN: If you will travel on the cheap. . . . On the first class deck the sun is shining at the rate of ten and six an hour, darling.

KAK: I say, Captain, where are the rest of the passengers?

CAPTAIN: There are no other passengers.

MATE: What's all this about?

Music suddenly stops. Everybody stands rock still. Dead silence.

CAPTAIN: (*shouting*) I beg to inform you the radiation sickness has left us the sole survivors of the human race.

PLASTIC MAC MAN enters obscured from head to foot in one mass of balloons, holding a fly swatter and lengths of coloured elastic.

PLASTIC MAC MAN: Arthur . . . Arthur . . . Arthur. . . . (*He distributes strips of elastic to all the cast, screaming*) They should never have invented rubber . . . rubber . . . stretching its sinful way round the world . . . those black rubber transparent women's macs . . . rubber girdles and douches . . . rubber waterproof sheets encouraging children to wet the beds when there's pots in the room.

MATE: 'Ere . . . you vote Socialist and we'll get rid of them rubber monopolies. . . .

PLASTIC MAC MAN: So, they're making the rubber monopolies now. . . . Ahh, it was the hand and foot and teeth, elbows, knees of God that dropped the . . . Bomb.

Sound of mule blowing raspberries. The cast fly into a panic, screaming 'The bomb, the bomb, the bomb' . . . and run all over the stage. MATE goes to mangle and puts 'hand' (this is a false rubber hand identical to his own) through rollers. CAPTAIN puts on parrot's beak and bib, takes up perch, acts like parrot. KAK beats bird with pillow, SEAMAN beats stage with his club, PENELOPE looks on with amazement. COFFIN MAN waves Union Jack and starts to paddle his coffin with a canoe paddle.

KAK : The 'H' Bomb.

PLASTIC MAC MAN : That's the one. On this sinful rubber civilisation. Stretch, brothers, and repent. Stretch and repent. . . .

MATE : Do as he says, he's a holy man. . . .

PLASTIC MAC MAN : Stretch and repent. . . . (*He says this repeatedly and rhythmically*)

Everyone stretches and repents, while the PLASTIC MAC MAN sings.

OMNES : Stretch and repent. (*Repeat*)

PLASTIC MAC MAN :
Oh, you dirty young devil, how dare you presume
To wet in the bed when the po's in the room.
I'll wallop your bum with a dirty great broom
When I get up in the morning time. . . .

The cast joins in reprise. End of reprise breaks into Irish jig. During jig, FORTNUM interrupts. FORTNUM is standing on the piano rostrum and dressed in long underwear and old Army cardigan. PIANIST is dressed in long underwear, Bahamas hat and dark glasses and angel's wings.

FORTNUM: Stop in the name of the Lord! (*Thunder and lightning*)

Sound: Great crash of thunder — very fierce.
Lights: In the whole theatre on and off. Above FORTNUM a golden light shines down from heaven. There is a pause in the thunder.

FORTNUM: Hark ye, the day of judgment is at hand.

Thunder and lightning. The cast is startled. All go on knees.

CAPTAIN: It's God!

MATE: Good old God. (*Sings*) For he's a jolly good fellow. (*Turns and encourages audiënce*) For he's . . . (*Breaks*) He's a Socialist, you know.

FORTNUM: Quiet, Labour scum!

KAK: Wait a minute . . . you don't look like God. You look like an ordinary mortal.

FORTNUM: I also do impressions.

CAPTAIN: O, save me, Lord God, from the dreadful death by radiation.

PLASTIC MAC MAN : Save me, merciful Lord, from the terrible temptations and perversions of the rubber. . . .

SEAMAN : Oh Lord . . . give me higher wages and a shorter working week. . . .

MATE : God, save me . . . and I'll give up being an atheist . . . Goddy . . .

PENELOPE : God ! Give me back my baby !

Silence. All look slowly at PENELOPE.

FORTNUM : Er . . . Yea, verily, in the fullness of time, the fruits of the ship shall be added unto you. . . .

MATE : See ! See !

Celestial music on a glockenspeil.

FORTNUM : *Now,* owing to the extreme radiation in these celestial altitudes . . . we are establishing the Kingdom of Heaven on earth in number twenty-nine Cul-de-Sac Place, Paddington . . . no coloureds or children.

CAPTAIN : O Lord . . . merciful Lord . . . how *shall* I reside in thy kingdom ?

FORTNUM : By paying a purely nominal rent of fifty guineas a week.

MATE : I'll pay it . . . I'll pay it. . . .

KAK leaps to his feet.

KAK: Wait a minute. That isn't God. . . . That is Lord Fortnum, the well-known bed-sitting room.

CAPTAIN grabs KAK and shakes him.

CAPTAIN: Blasphemer!

CAPTAIN and KAK fight on the bed.

FORTNUM: That's right. Captain, kill him!

CAPTAIN: Oh God, oh God, say the word . . . and I'll punch him in the throat. . . . (*To KAK*) Recant . . . recant, you shameful blasphemer!

All below performed ad lib.

PLASTIC MAC MAN: Arthur . . . Arthur . . . Arthur. . . . (*Sings again*) Oh you dirty old devil, how dare you presume, etc.

Remainder of cast dance happily around stage. MATE throws money up to God. PENELOPE looks on.

SEAMAN: (*rings his ship's telegraph and shouts*) Higher wages, God!

KAK: (*shouts through loud hailer*) Lord Fortnum, as your doctor, I must strongly advise against the taking of prayer! And money and sugar.

MATE: You look after me and I'll look after you, Goddy, I got more stashed away in a biscuit tin.

We hear the sound of a baby crying. The chaotic din dies away. They fall silent in surprise. Then slowly they all approach the cot and look down into it. Lights start to dim. Cot is spot-lit. KAK gives a toothy bewildered smile, finds the rattle and shakes it over the cot. MATE looks at baby, bewildered, looks at God, looks back at baby, and then to God again.
Black out — spot on FORTNUM's face. Spot from above on group around baby. Music over loudspeakers: Choir — 'The First Noel'.

THE END